A Mind to Work

A Mind to Work

✦

The Life and Career Planning Guide for People Who Need to Work!

Francina R. Harrison

iUniverse, Inc.
New York Lincoln Shanghai

A Mind to Work
The Life and Career Planning Guide for People Who Need to Work!

iUniverse, Inc.

For information address:
iUniverse, Inc.
2021 Pine Lake Road, Suite 100
Lincoln, NE 68512
www.iuniverse.com

ISBN: 0-595-30390-0

First and foremost, I thank GOD for the vision, direction of my life and the completion of this work. There are so many friends and family members that I must acknowledge who have helped me along the way. I thank GOD for my husband, Tonnie. Your foundational faith, unwavering spirit and peaceful countenance got us through 13 years of life experience. To my children, Nehemiah and To'niah, you are the future and I thank GOD for blessing me with such wonderful seeds, thank you two for your patience. To my parents, Jonathan and Ettishia Goode for giving me life and the foundation that enabled me to write this book. To my sisters, Shawna Goode and Paula Goode, (Grantham), my best friends Fern Webb, Christopher Gary and future brother-in-law Ray Grantham—thanks for the encouragement/prayers. (Ray, welcome to the family.)

To my kinfolk, the people who I call family you all deserve a push-up and round of applause: **My North Carolina Family**: George Barfield Senior, Joyce Barfield-Graham, Angelia Barfield-Bremby, Shirley Barfield-Gillis, Uncle Bill Barfield and Uncle George Barfield III. All of my aunts, uncles, cousins who represent The Kinston, NC Barfield Family.

My Connecticut family: Emily and Reginald Robinson, Katherine Franklin, Les, Esther, Sarah and Megan Morrel, Bennie and Mildred Jennings, Pastor Benjamin, K. Watts and the Shiloh Baptist Church Family.

My Virginia Family: Mr. Booker T. and Lenora (Ms. Shug) Smith, Mr. Alvin and Hortense Williams, Kathy Easley and family, Barbara Spence, David and Gail Hamilton, PanShiela Cole and all members of the Job Network Ministry and my super, super personal editors: Latoya Gilbert and Tiffany Jones. You two are awesome, don't ever forget that and Pastors William D. and Joyce Scott (and my church family) of the Pleasant Grove Baptist Church of Virginia Beach, VA.

My South Carolina Family: Dr. Nathaniel and Mary Lee Wilder, and all of my 16 brother and sister-in-laws: Lucille, Mae, Barbara, Queen, Gloria, Marie, Mary Ann, Marilyn, Lorraine, and Minnie (GOD rest her soul), Isaiah, Edward, L.B. (wherever you are), Sonny, John, Joseph and the late Joyce Marie Harrison (mother to us all).

Last but not least, I want to thank all of the people who have touched my life with "Power Statements" and quotes. Thank you for your wisdom.

Contents

Foreword

There are many things that we will share on our journey towards a life of purpose, so I need for you to know something. This book is designed to give you some immediate tools for a new change process. I have included "Power Statements" which are phrases or sayings that I have used within the last 20 years from my daily walk of life. As you read each section, think about the "Power Statements" and how they can apply to your situation. I also suggest that you have a composition book or journal handy (life journal) to record or start your daily life entries. I will be giving you "life work" and will often refer you to using your journal to coincide with that particular lesson. I believe in a well-equipped toolbox, consider the power statements and your life journal your tools for life. There will be several questions asked of you in this book. You will use your Life Journal to answer, brainstorm and script your power statements. Let's begin. To set the tone for this powerful process, I would like to share a poem with you that starts with this question in mind: *Who's in your front row?*

Life is a theater-invite your audience carefully. Not
everyone is healthy enough to have a front row seat in
our lives. There are some people in your life that need
to be loved from a distance.

It's amazing what you can accomplish when you let go,
or at least minimize, your time with draining,
negative, incompatible, not-going-anywhere
relationships/friendships.

Observe the relationships around you. Pay attention.

Which ones lift and which ones lean? Which ones
encourage and which ones discourage? Which ones are on

a path of growth uphill and which ones are going downhill?

When you leave certain people, do you feel better or feel worse? Which ones always have drama or don't really understand, know or appreciate you?

The more you seek quality, respect, growth, peace of mind, love and truth around you, the easier it will become for you to decide who gets to sit in the **front row** and who should be moved to the balcony of your life.

Remember that people we hang with will have an impact on both our lives and income. And so we must be careful to choose the people we hang out with, as well as the information with which we feed our minds. We should not share our dreams with negative people, nor feed them with negative thoughts.

Who's in your front row?

—*Author Unknown, www.hearangelswhisper.com* (Sunshine Page of Inspiration)

It's All About You!

It begins with you! Yes, definitely with you. You have opened the pages of this book, looking for new insights or techniques to cure the pain of today. You may be asking yourself, how can I find something helpful to use in my life to create the life designs of my dreams? Perhaps you are not satisfied, fulfilled or living without purpose or direction. Well, I say again, it begins with you. Are you willing to make the ultimate sacrifice; take healthy risks and believe in that which is not seen? Are you willing to be brave enough to discover new depths of your being? Are you willing to go to those places of hurt, shame, and betrayal? Yes, even there!

If you have answered yes to at least one of the above questions, then you are ready for your journey to that place of self-discovery, a new tomorrow, and a brighter today. Together we will go to that place where you are walloped in self-confidence and the ultimate acceptance of who you are. More than that, you will have discovered something about who you are and where you belong. These fundamental findings will evidence themselves in your whole self, the emotional, the physical and the spiritual you. This book is just for you! Designed with you in mind, in an effort to allow you the permission to respect yourself, embrace your uniqueness and honor your spirit. However, I find it totally necessary to place a disclaimer at this point of the text. You may be so immersed in the regeneration of your soul that you may find yourself in places you never dared go to before. Change starts within; come with me to embrace faith, understand power and finally the ability to really discover...you.

Now I have been known to be a cynic, I am sure questions are being raised regarding what does power, faith, respect, self-discovery and risk taking have to do with the employment process? Well, I am glad you asked. From this moment forward, I want you to recite and begin to believe that it's deeper than a job. The conversation is about you and whether you know who you are and what you bring. This book is designed with two parts; the first part will address and prepare *you* in your career search/life mission process. The second part of this book will provide you with the technical abilities that you gathered from the first few chapter to propel you into self-power and competence during your career search. We shall begin the process of building a solid foundation (spirit, emotional and physical) and maintaining that foundation. Once the foundation has been laid, your power (and that's what it is) will manifest. You will find a direct link with your earthly purpose, life mission, and a place of contentment that goes beyond all understanding. It's all there; inside you, however, not in its proper place. We will find your order together, finding that right vocation that meets your life purpose.

Let me reiterate the importance of the life journal, for the change process, as mentioned in the Foreword of this book. Nothing fancy, a simple composition or notebook will suffice as your life journal. You will find that this tool will prove useful in brainstorming and tapping into your gifts, talents, interests and undeveloped strengths. Another tool used throughout this book are the *power statements,* which are phrases, and/or sayings that I have used for my own change process. These statements have not been derived from books, articles, or the usual forms of documentation. What's fascinating about these thoughts are that they were shared with me by *everyday hardworking Americans—the backbone of our society*...people just like you. These power statements were shared in the lunchroom, at the kitchen table, on the subway, at the barbershop, during church services and at work. When possible, I have included the names and dates of the person who first shared these thoughts or life strategies with me. Now it's my turn to share them with you. So from this moment on, open your mind, and take the first step if you want different results. Are you ready? Let's start at the beginning.

In The Beginning (Everything has a starting point)

I remember taking a biology class in college where we were studying the human creation process. One thing that stuck in my mind was that as a human being is created in the womb, it begins from the top (brain) to the bottom, then from the middle out to the rest of the organism. Let me clarify. A medical professional I'm not; however, the significance of this for our purposes of self-discovery is that you have to start at the top then work your way down. We all know the story of creation found in the Bible, the Book of Genesis 1:1: "In the beginning GOD created the heavens and the earth." According to this scripture, GOD did not create the earth first, then the heavens, but the other way around. Medical example follows suit during the conception process; it starts at the brain and works its way to the rest of the body. Here comes the human fallacy; we don't feel that it's necessary to follow nature's process. That would be too time-consuming. We life forms have decided that we can purchase a new suit; snappy shoes, great hair do and that will do the job. Not! This is a working process and you are a work in progress. Every good work has to have a beginning, and in terms of this book, the beginning is you.

Power Statement No. 1

Change your attitude; you will change your life.

—Barbara Jones, 2000

Let us start at our beginning. You know, the big "A" word. **Attitude.** This may be the single most important step for our entire journey. As I said earlier, it begins with you. Clear your mind, right now, empty out all the clutter, labels, name calling, and childhood memories that bring about ill feelings of self. Empty your clutter, now! We need to have a clear mind and your commitment to only allow positive ideas/images to root. This is a requirement, not a request. Now, we will begin the process of foundation building with thoughts and recitations that will initiate the refueling process. Let's set our foundation building process right now. Whenever you see a power statement, such as the one above, recite it to yourself three times. Twice orally while looking at the words. Once silently with your eyes closed slowly seeing the phrase in your mind's eye. This will be the routine for every power statement from this point on.

Now back to attitude. Let's start thinking about how we want to be. Answer the following: Do you want to be happy, content, successful, full of hope, strengthened by faith…a genuine work of art? It's okay. Visualize your dreams, dream out loud, and say what you want. (As an aside, it's okay to talk to yourself, it's healthy; I do it all the time.) In your journal, write these items down. Just start scribbling, no order, and list all your wants at this point. Are you being real with yourself? There is a scriptural truth that if you can conceive it, it can be achieved. Are you seeing it? Write it down. You may have seen this idea in Covey's principle "Begin with the End in Mind" from his book *The 7 Habits of Highly Effective People.* I bring this up because I think it's very important to acknowledge that truth is truth (no matter where you read it).

Power Statement No. 2

Define yourself or be defined.

—Diane Williams, 1997

If you want the world to receive you in a certain way, hopefully some of the ways you listed in your journal, you must set the tone. The power is resting with you, why don't you use it? If you want respect, command it; if you want honesty, don't tolerate dishonesty; if you want truth, don't be happy with lies, and only respond to the name that was given to you. People will treat you the way you allow them to. Define yourself! If you don't, society will; for many of us, society already has. You have heard some of the words, slow, dumb, female (instead of woman), male (instead of man), dislocated worker, unemployed, disabled, dysfunctional...I think you get my point.

Let's not forget our part in the above labeling process (a.k.a. self-labels). Many of us find comfort in those labels and are the first to use that category to describe ourselves. We have eagerly embraced the terminology, limits, and lifestyle associated with life stealing labels. I don't mean to burst your spirit, but in the words of the late Malcolm X, as stated in Iyanla Vanzant's, book *Acts of Faith* "You've been tricked! You've been had! Hoodwinked! Bamboozled!" (Page 2/26). Define yourself or be defined; there is more to you than a label and limits. You need to set your tone, know your name and set your expectations. I don't even want to go to those other words that people have responded to, well let me give you a hint to name a few: the female dog, the other word for prostitute and the "N" word. Ladies and gentlemen, from this moment on, please resist from responding to the above-mentioned jargon, no matter how *down* it is. Now let me correct myself, if you are one of those things, please respond—accordingly. Then the world and I will know exactly how you want to be treated.

Power Statement No. 3

As a man thinks so he is.

—Old Testament, *Proverbs* 23:7

I find it interesting that I can walk around a room or down a street, observant of all that is around me, smiling and talking with people as I walk by. There I am, a body in motion, without the faintest clue of how my body functions without my conscious execution. If I decide to walk forward, my body executes thousands of commands for me to complete this task. If I decide to stop, the previous commands cease and subordinate to new ones. This is the power of the mind (thinking) and direction (action) to achieve a goal. What's the point? In order for my body to move forward, my brain needs to execute a command, a decision, and some type of direction. The conscious body cannot go contrary to the brain's command; the body is an action agent for the brain to direct. If you want happiness, act as if you are happy. If you want to be organized, act as if you are organized. If you want satisfaction, act as if you are satisfied. If you want to be employed, act as if you are employable.

Your mind and body have to be on the same page. In fact, many of us have been using this principle for years, just in its negative fashion. Don't believe me, try this out: think negative thoughts, think hopelessness, think unloved/unable, or think lonely. Are you feeling these purpose killers? Are you tired of feeling this way; you can stop it. Think, *I can*. Think *possibilities*. Think *overcomer*. Think, *I am not alone and think I can do this…now!*

Power Statement No. 4

> *If it's in the root, it's going to show up in the fruit.*
> —**Rev. William D. Scott, Sermon, 1998**

Life doesn't get any simpler than this. It doesn't take much to figure people out, just look at their works. My elders have a saying: "You will know a tree by the fruit it bears." We need to constantly develop our observations and research skills, yes for the employment market and for life in general. We walk around being consumed with anger toward people who have fulfilled their root mission, they bear fruit. Our anger continues to manifest, we become so deeply wounded, and keep those wounds open for years. Then give the victimizers some salt, help them shake the salt into our wounds, yell and scream in pain…then go back for more! This behavior is a cycle of insanity. This behavior is affecting your creation of self and attitude; you can't put your best foot forward when you are wounded. Find some better trees to hang around if the fruit you taste is rotten. There are plenty of trees out there with excellent fruit. If we would take the time to wait and see, our emotional, spiritual and physical taste buds will be delighted with a sweet nectar that would yield more good fruit when planted. What are you saying? Research and build a power packed network. Look at your tree, assess your associates and your family; if the fruit is rotten…stay away from the tree (or plant a new one).

Power Statement No. 5.

> *Your attitude determines your altitude.*
> —**Rev. William D. Scott, Sermon, 1995**

Want a straight way to failure? Keep a dysfunctional attitude. You will fail for sure. If you want to stay down there with misery, incompetence, less than, and *but's*, keep your negative attitude and the behaviors that support these goals. You will remain a footstool or doormat for society to walk on. Believe me, society, will wear the pointiest heels and the dirtiest boots as they step on top of you on their way to the top. If you like it at the bottom, then stay there. You are intelligent. I know that because you are reading this book in search of change. You want what's yours. You want to go higher in your purpose; I applaud you for looking up. If you have to look somewhere, don't look around—always look up. As your attitude elevates, so will your potentials. Don't be afraid to discover your purpose or to accept change. Stay focused, always looking up. Here is an exercise for you, lift you head up right now. What do you see? At first response you will probably say; a ceiling or the sky, look again. What do you see directly above your head? I hope the answer is nothing! My point is there is no lid or cover above your head, you are not living in a glass jar and there is nothing locking you down. You have the power of creation; creation comes from nothing. When you have nothing, create!

Power Statement No. 6

You have been given two guarantees—one is life the other is death; what you do in between is totally up to you!

—1992

Nobody owes you anything. That's right, I said it. The world owes you nothing. Your friends owe you nothing, and your significant other definitely owes you nothing. If you are in a relationship where you are confused (he/she owes me versus true love), you are living beneath your purpose. If you have confused needs versus wants in a relationship, you are in the direct path of emotional suicide. Just for the record, science has determined that the human body needs the following items to sustain itself: food, water, and oxygen. Everything else is negotiable. Ladies and gentlemen, if you get nothing else out of this book, please walk away understanding that everything outside of the food, water and oxygen is manageable.

The status of your life right now is based on the sum of actions, thoughts, perceptions, fears, risk and personal direction that you have allowed. If you don't like where you are, or what you are, do something about it! If you want to truly blame someone for where you are, go right now into the bathroom, look in the mirror and take it out on that individual that is staring right back at you. After all, it's that person's fault, not yours. On this big blue planet, we have received two earthly promises, life and death. We have been given a breath of life. We were born naked and naked we shall return. Our other guarantee is coming; we will surely die.

All of the time in between life and death is up to us. At this point, you may be asking yourself, why have I said all of this, what is my point? Simply this, stop the blame and denial game. All it will produce is stopping your process toward a life of your dreams. Stop pointing fingers, accept responsibility now and get into your game. If you have followed the above power statements, I am hopeful that you have opened your mind to the possibilities of you. I am also hopeful that you realize that you can now stop the name-the-blame game, stop fishing in De Nile, and take back all the power you have given away. Choose life now. Reach for a powerful life that is in line with your ordained purpose.

Power Statement No. 7

If nothing changes, nothing changes.

—**Dr. Moore, Sermon, 1995**

Are you understanding how important choice is yet? Here is the last segment on rebuilding our attitudes. I am sure you have heard the older people say, "You get out of it what you put into it." This is true in attitude building and life direction. If you have chosen to stay the same, and yet expecting different results; you are mistaken. The earlier principles have stated that an action element is paramount in life designing. However, if you are totally satisfied with where you are, then stay there. Just remember this, if your life's desire is to remain the same, please don't complain, you'll become a real bore and a pain. (Wow, that's my first and last rhyme in this book.) I say that with genuine concern, we must tell the truth and yes, sometimes the truth hurts, but it will set you free.

Where Do I Belong?

Power Statement No. 8

Know who you are and what you bring.

—Dr. Joseph Dancy, Classroom Lecture, 1995

We shared this thought in the previous section on attitude: it is imperative that we begin the process of honesty with ourselves. As I said earlier, the truth may hurt, but it will set you free. In discovering the best environment for us to work in, we must know and commit to discovering who we are and what we bring. We can begin this process by asking a few simple questions that you'll find listed below (use your life journal):

- Who am I?

- What makes me smile or frown?

- What do I dream about?

- Who do I admire most, and why?

- What makes me tick?

- What are the skeletons in my closet?

- What are my unresolved issues?

- What environments would I NOT want to work in, list three of them?

- List three things I like about myself.

- List five things I would like to change about myself.

Sometimes it's difficult to rate ourselves. The next set of questions involves the others in our lives who may be willing to tell the real truth. (Yes, this is another life journal moment)

- What would my mother want to change about me?

- How would my mother describe me?

- How would my best friend describe me?

- What would my spouse or significant other say I need to work on?

Do you see the pattern? Ask yourself questions that will get to the heart of you: your soul, your belly…the deepest places of your being. If you don't know you, you can't go forward with this process. Trust the process and trust yourself, go on, discover who you are (I dare you)!

As your discovery starts opening up rivers of knowledge, write them down in your journal. Write everything down in two groups: my strengths and my under-developed strengths. Be real with yourself regarding items you need to work on. You have your hard skills: knowledge bases of computer applications, keyboarding speed, languages, and machinery tools (in short, items outside of yourself). Then you have your soft skills or the skills that make you uniquely human: communication, interpersonal skills, team player, work ethic, etc. When you start knowing and believing in all the gifts and talents that you possess, then you can start brainstorming on the environments where your gifts and talents can be used in relation to your purpose.

Power Statement No. 9

> *Dream out loud-where do you want to go; a dream can help get you there.*

> **—Sylvia, 1996**

I am sure you are saying to yourself, "she has lost it." What do you mean dream out loud? We only dream while we are sleeping. I agree, we do start the dream process while we are in the solitude of sleep. Our minds and bodies are finally at rest from the reactions of our daily lives. Perhaps we have even found a quiet and peaceful distance that has allowed us to dream. We allow ourselves to enter in remarkable places, receive awesome visions, and receive directions from our supernatural realms. However, we then allow that reducer of time, the alarm clock to awaken us from our sweet serenity to revisit the daily routine of work, hustle and pay. For most of us the buzz of the alarm terminates our dream process. Many times we forget the possibilities that were shared in our spirit. When we awake, we find that our focus returns to the here and now, versus the tomorrow and then. The short word in all of this is the big G-word…goals. We must have goals, a path or map if you would, to a specific destination. You remember what our elders have said, "If you don't know where you are going, how do you plan to get there?" Many of us are stuck in the here and now, and have forgotten to set goals. Here are some questions that you may want to ask yourself in the goal defining process (Journal Time!):

- What are the top five things (concepts) that are important to me?

- Where do I want to be in one, five, ten, and 20 years?

- What type of home do I want? (dream big)

- What legacy do I want to leave for my children?

- What is my dream job (the work I would do for free)?

Those are the hard concepts or tangibles (things we can touch or feel). However, I have found it just as important to dream about the intangibles in life. Here are some questions to ask yourself:

- What would it take to make me happy and to love my job?

- How do I see myself now?

- What five items do I want to change about myself?

- What five things do I need to change in myself? What will it take for me to be satisfied?

- How will I know that I'm satisfied?

- What is my purpose?

- When I leave this earth, what are the (3) items that I wish people would have known about me? (My fears kept me from telling them in the living.)

Now is the time to get real with yourself about your goals. What is important? What would make you happy and where do you want to go? Lose that entitlement mindset and transform your thinking into empowerment. Webster defines empowerment as "to give official authority or legal power to, to promote the self-actualization or influence of." (2003 edition) The power is within, and most of it starts with mental conditioning. As stated in the beginning of this book your life is your responsibility, go for it. Design the life you want for yourself. Will set backs or tribulations come? Of course! Do you let situations stop you from your dream? If you have allowed set backs to keep you from your dream in the past here is what you need to do. In terms of your past set backs, put a period there, two spaces, and start a new paragraph (just like you are typing a new page). You have the power; decide to use it. Today.

Power Statement No. 10

I'm Tired of Surviving, I Want to Live.

—**Donna, 1997**

In my academic studies, I had the privilege of working with a variety of people from different walks, backgrounds, and struggles. One day I was observing a group session in a residential program for persons who met the following three criteria: substance abusers, mentally ill and homeless (and you thought you had it bad). This was a very challenging group for persons who really had a hard time meeting life on life's terms. During this session, many members were showcasing their routine pity parties, using the blame/denial game versus movement towards personal empowerment. I figured, I would do my observations, not expecting any magic moments and wait for the end of the hour.

Then at one moment a female group member who I will name Donna, gently rose her head from a defeated position, looked at the other members in the group with a sense of disdain, and softly said, "I am tired of surviving, I want to live." At that particular moment, an eerie silence fell over the group. Many of the members looked at Donna with surprise. Donna did not only have the three attributes listed in the beginning of this text: addiction, mental illness, and homelessness; she was also HIV positive and having severe medical struggles. Many of the group members considered Donna a walking cemetery. How could she talk about living, when she has been given a bona fide death sentence? I too was in shock at Donna's statement, many of the members had isolated Donna due to the fear of her HIV status and possible threat of full-blown AIDS.

ᖯ   Once she made her **statement of determination** and actually verbalized her statement; the obvious became real. Donna persevered that day. Once she made up her mind, her body and actions followed. Donna immediately put an action-oriented plan into place that began with a focus on living. One of the first things she did was change her appearance. Her previous look embodied death and destruction. Her outlook no longer fit her transformed mindset. She restored the beauty that was always there. She began to actively participate in her recovery program. She enrolled in several programs at the facility to prepared for life re-entry (work, housing, family). Donna obtained a part-time job in the facility and that work component gave her a renewed vigor and belief that anything was possible.

In Donna's case, not only was her statement of determination necessary, but also we find that Donna's working was therapeutic! Getting up with a purpose, putting your life back together and knowing that you have choices and the power to choose, equates to living. What's my point? Why would I share this story about this mentally diagnosed, chronically depressed, homeless, HIV patient? What could we possibly have in common with someone like *that?* (Let me state for the record that this experience occurred when the HIV epidemic was still very new to the heterosexual world.) After all this is a "job hunting" book; why would I need to hear all of this? My answer? It's important to know what is possible. This example gives us one out of thousands of examples of people who find their purpose, or life mission, under circumstances that would scare your soul. It gives you an opportunity to understand and get the point that you can do this. The bottom line is that if you free your mind, the rest (or the buttisimo) will follow.

Power Statement No. 11

I will get on top of my struggle.

—Ms. Freeman, 1997

Are you struggling right now? Is there a monkey on your back, as the older people would say? Is there something toying with your mind to keep you from a peaceful existence? If you answered yes to any of the above questions, our blue ribbon task force of the nation's best behavior heath providers has determined that you are struggling. By the way there is no task force, that was a joke, so lighten-up. However, good old-fashioned common sense tells us that the above feelings of mental exhaustion, constant stress and anxiety are evidence that in some parts of our lives we are having a tug of war. The worst part of our particular tug of war is that no one is winning. Our life rope is being pulled at both ends and there we are in the middle standing in mud.

Here is the good news; this too shall pass. These feelings, or this situation, will not last forever. You can beat this! Would you like to know how? First admit to yourself out loud that you are having a struggle. In order to correct something, we must first admit that there is something to correct. Remember that our definition of a struggle is a person, place, or thing that we have allowed to take our personal power from us. This is an item that is keeping us from reaching our fullest potential, our personal, professional goals and genuine happiness. Let's get real with ourselves. The struggle may be a man, a woman, money, food, showing up late or not at all, limited vocabulary, critical spirit, combative spirit, no spirit, mediocrity, or complacency. Let's go deeper, other struggles that inhibit our growth are: our self-image, self-esteem, anger, judgmental attitudes, victim hood, and failure to accept responsibility.

In my opinion, the most potentially dangerous struggles are the ones that are undeniably ours, yet we fail to accept that ownership. The first step is to recognize our participation in activities that deny our responsibility. An example of such participation is playing the blame and denial game-blaming other people for where you are. Here are some examples of those "I refuse to acknowledge my contribution to my life" statements:

- It's his/her fault for treating me that way.

- She made me do it.

- I did not have any choice.

- I want to…but I can't.

- They said I shouldn't do that.

- Okay, if you say so.

- I was going to tell him/her/them how I feel, but…

Have I missed any other statements? Hopefully, you get where I am coming from. The second step; if you catch yourself using any of these excuses/reasons…just simply stop yourself and say, "I will get and stay on top of that struggle."

The third step, once you have admitted and accepted your contribution to your struggle, is action. What are some action steps that you can do, individually, to manage your struggle? Understand this, the only behavior that you can change is your behavior. Stop the fallacy of expecting people to change for you. You know how resistant to change you are, so how would you expect someone else to change for you? Let me get back on point, the third point that is. Attack this struggle verbally. Repeat the power statement when you feel yourself going there. In the appendix of this book are several power statements for everyday use to keep you focused. Establish a ritual in your household that starts with a statement of power from that list. This will keep you on top of the struggle instead of the struggle being on top of you. Let me bring this point home, the struggle does not just blink away, no magic wands here. But day by day, as your action-oriented plan goes into effect, make sure the struggle is under you and not over you. Think of your situation as a mathematic fraction, $(I/struggle)$.

Most of our stress comes, and feels unbearable, when the struggle is in the numerator and we have become the denominator. Struggle/You = chaos. Your task is to develop and manage a plan that keeps the following: You/Struggle = you are in control. This is all about reclaiming your power. You need to be willing to tell yourself that enough is enough. Here are some statements that may help you pause the defeating behaviors and set the tone for designing new ones. Yes, this may be a good time for the life journal to record and expound on statements that hit home with you.

- I deserve better than this.

- I am disgusted with my decision-making.

- What makes me feel so inadequate?

- I am okay; there is nothing wrong with me.

- How could I have allowed these setbacks/struggles to put my life on pause.

- I am not perfect and I am okay with that.

- I am much better than this.

- I am a good person and you can't keep a good man/woman down.

This process could take several hours, several days or longer. This is a definite crossroads point for you. I am asking you to get real with yourself, no matter what others think, feel or even say about you. This is a place of bravery and courage. Now is the time to visit that place where you have hidden your secrets and deal with those demons that haunt you. If you are able to handle your demons on your own, great. If you believe that you need help in sorting out your demons, then get it. I believe in you, now its time for you to believe in yourself.

Once you have undergone this crucial step, set the stage for rebuilding. You have accepted responsibility and now you are ready for the next step. This next step is so important and is definitely the magnet for change. Here it is: **just stop it**. This sounds so simple doesn't it? Just stop the behavior that keeps you from soaring. Now, the feelings may not stop immediately, those may take time. However, you can cease all physical actions that initiate and keep the struggle fires burning. Do you think I am being too simple? Well, let's give it a try. Let's say that your struggle involves a person, someone who you have given power to control or direct your life. Perhaps you have let this person manipulate your work, family or personal goals.

Because you have made your statement of determination to design your life, now this person has demanded or requested an action from you. The new you will simply respond, "No." There is no need to react to conversations with negative language or intimidations. You don't need to react to everything that is said about you. I mean, if someone calls you, as people would say, *out of your name*, are you that thing which has been called? If so, then respond. However, I believe that you are more than that and true strength comes in not responding to nonsense.

Now on a very serious note, there may be several persons who are reading this book and you may be involved in dangerous personal relationships. By no means are you to perform any of these tasks towards a person who has threatened you with bodily harm. The power and control issues that I am primarily referring to in this book are those of a non-violent nature where no threat or evidence of harm exists. If you are finding yourself in a family violence situation, you should seek the appropriate help immediately and contact your local family violence authorities, especially if you feel that your life may be in danger. If you are not in this situation, count your blessings, and let's continue with our work.

The same response would be relevant for those items or places that have your power. If you are a late bloomer (someone who is always late), say "no" to lack of planning and set yourself to be 30 minutes earlier at all events. Just get up and move one hour earlier than usual. If a place is holding you back, don't go there anymore. Find other places to raise your level of experiences, or somewhere you have never been before where all your senses can be stimulated. Find some new places that radiate positivity. Besides, a change of scenery is a good thing.

Each time you say and do "no" you will begin to stir something up on the inside that will be evident on the outside. The first words of this book were "It begins with you." If you want to be successful, you have to renegotiate your place in this world and define who you are and what you bring. It's okay to expect the best and not settle for anything less. Settling is the trick of comfortability to keep you from your divine gifts and purposes. You have the power to live your life and declare now and forevermore…struggle, you are my footstool and I will worship you no more!

Power Statement No. 12

Man, I want to be like Mike!

—Verbal reference to Michael Jordan, 1995

I don't remember where I was when I heard this quote. Mr. Jordan was performing in his awesome fashion on the basketball court. All eyes were on him. I remember the roaring applause, the cheering voices and the expressions of awe on every young face. Some wanted his talent. Some wanted his fame. Others wanted the respect on the court. Michael? He was just being Michael, playing the game that he loved. This brought to mind a question once asked in a Superman movie: "Is a bird showing off when he flies?" Certainly, the answer is no. Those of us in transition have to learn how to find and play our game. Understand that getting to your real game requires much work. The initial way to do this is to find a person, your own Mike, who has attained a level of success or perfection in his/their game that meets your dream. I am going to put this out there; I hope your Mike or Flojo is a person of good taste and moral fortitude who has stood the test of time. I also am hopeful that we have gone past those external factors and are looking towards the stuff of substance. If not, re-read this chapter.

The Bible gives an example of role modeling and states that when Jesus found disciples he said follow me. (Bible, Matthew 9:9). They immediately stopped what they were doing and followed him, literally and figuratively. They listened to his words, developed values, codes of conduct and self-discipline, received education and wisdom over time. This is a true definition of a role model, someone that we look up to; maybe think about imitating. If the art of imitation will keep you focused on achieving your goals, then imitate. When you are getting ready to plan a course of action, ask yourself, "what would _____do? Would he/she cut corners, work harder or go for perfection? Be careful in this measure, I am not saying to forget all about you and pretend to be someone else. I want you to be the best you that you can be. I believe the role model project can help jump start your goals process and maintain a focus. Remember, success takes work. It requires discipline, focus and desire (the fuel from the heart). Model your behavior after someone you admire, someone of substance that you look up to. Remember, "Man, I want to be like Mike", but always be you.

Power Statement No. 13

Making a Living Is Not The Same as Making a Life.

—**Rev. Moore, 1999**

Yes, this may be the part where the money comes in. What is important to you, what is your motivation? Are you in it solely for the money? We all need, as they say in the Corrections industry at least "three hots and a cot" to maintain our existence. I know you can't smile and go into your local grocery store, get a cart full of groceries just because you are cute. However, don't put the cart before the horse. Find that *thing* you love to do…the *thing* that people compliment you on, the *thing* you can do in your sleep. Remember the dream out loud project earlier where we talked about all of our wants, thoughts and desires? Our vocational purposes should be in direct relation to our life missions. You want to be successful in your career? Find what you love to do and do it well. This could be your vocation; the very *thing* you love to do so much you would do it for free.

When your work is a labor of love, your rewards will be substantial. The money will come; in fact, this is the best way to get paid. Work in the *thing* that you love to do. When we work in the industry that we enjoy, we tend to have incredible measurable outcomes that increase, seemingly without effort, such as production, quality, and customer satisfaction. It's a labor of love; in fact, it becomes part of you. Now that's the best scenario. Our goal is to help you get there. Have you ever felt that you are in the right place at the right time…that all the elements, time, opportunity, preparation etc, have all lined up in your favor? Some call this coincidence; I call it purpose filled intervention. That's what we want, to find our purpose and get paid for doing what we love. When we have achieved that, we have made the transition from improbable to possible and have created a mind to work.

Push-up, Pull-up and a Round Of Applause! (This Is Truly a State of Mind.)

Power Statement No. 14

"Push-up!"

—Ms. White, 1995

Anyone who knows me has heard me shout the late 90's slogan *push-up*. It just rolls off my tongue effortlessly when I have found an item of positivity that definitely requires a shout out. Like most words in the English language, this phrase has a literal and symbolic meaning. Let's look at the literal meaning of the word push: "to move against resistance; thrust" and the word up: "from a lower to a higher position, in, at or to a higher position" (Webster.com, 2003). In the physical sense, a push-up not only builds endurance but also strengthens the arms and upper body. Doing push-ups will toughen you and make you stronger.

Now you may be asking, "how does a push-up apply to my career and life pursuits?" In all of your doing, it is important that you remember to first give yourself a push-up, acknowledging the positive steps that you have made towards your life's designs. The push-up is a self-proclamation that you are expecting an elevation in your position and you will push to get there. It acknowledges positive works in your life and others; it builds self-esteem, self-reliance and self-preservation. Push-ups bring smiles and excitement. In short, it feels good and it's contagious. So whenever you hear a good thing, see a positive step, feel good feeling or achieve a goal (big/small) remember to say it with authority Push-up! Then actually push-up with your arms to the sky with your power praise. Let me remind you, this is a victory state of mind—no victims here. When times are tough, just remember the L.G.P. Principle: look up to get up, then push-up.

Power Statement No. 15

Pull-up! You are all to pieces.

—Ms. White, 1995

Now we know that in all things there is an opposite and/or counter effective movement. Even in the spirit of push-up we find ourselves at times being tragically human in our attempts toward change. And you know what, it's okay; I want all of us to strive for that perfect place. You know the saying, *shoot for the moon, if you miss, at least you will land on the stars.* The important word for all of us here is to never give up or give in. If we've lost our ability to push-up then flip the script and *pull-up.* If there is an area where you are stuck, or can't seem to get out of, it's time for you to pull yourself up. Now in the physical sense, a pull-up requires more work, use of more muscles and it's hard to do. Webster defines pull: "to apply force to in order to draw toward the force; tug at" (Webster.com, 2003). It may appear impossible at times, but you can pull-up, in fact you have to or you will miss your purpose.

As I have said in the beginning and will continue to the end, pull-up on the things that are keeping you down, depressed, and in emotional, spiritual and physical starvation. You may be asking yourself, "What are the things I should pull-up on?" Here are a few: settlement mentality, victim personality, loss of focus, poor attendance, negative attitude, self-hatred, longing for what you can't have, and unhealthy relationships. Do any of these apply to you? Are you performing any of these self-sabotaging behaviors right now? If so, pull-up now, before you drown in a well of self-pity, hopelessness and unrealized dreams. After all, these are your options; push, pull or stay still, you choose.

Power Statement No. 16

"...And a round of applause."

—F.R. Harrison, 1998

I don't want to start this section on such a sour note, so I will provide a push-up right now. While we are performing our exercises in order to get stronger, let's not forget to give ourselves a round of applause after we have performed our sets. You know, do a push-up, now a round of applause; do a pull-up and now a round of applause. When is the last time you had a round of applause to celebrate your accomplishment of the moment? Please do this: it will make our exercise of the mind go farther, faster, smoother and healthier. Now the essential question is

"What does this have to do with my work life?" Remember what I have said: this is deeper than a job. This is about you knowing who you are and what you bring. Push-up/pull-ups will make you stronger, keep you centered, and thicken your skin to deal with the obstacles in life. They will help you handle rejection and dissatisfactions without taking it personally. Push-ups/pull-ups will help you focus on what's really important, keep positivity in your life and delete those things that ensure death (spiritual and emotional that is). If you continue to look up and push in that direction, then you will go up.

Congratulations, you are now ready to go forward with the technical skills needed to obtain the career choice of your dreams. If you have made it to this point of the book, some real time and thought into purging and rejuvenation of your spirit has taken place. You have become real with who you are, no hustle or game. A real discovery of your gifts, talents, and purpose is at hand. Now, the easier work begins.

My Personal Career Search—It's Deeper Than a Job.

❖

Packaging and Response

Power Statement No. 17

I am the CEO of Me Inc.

—Mr. Williams, 1998

From this moment on think of yourself as a business. You are a for profit organization with a product line, body of knowledge and expertise in your area of concentration. In fact, let's verbally bring this into reality. State your business name, now (examples: Harrison & Associates, The Harrison Group, Harrison Enterprises). Find a mirror right now and look directly at yourself, smile and state "I am the CEO of (state your business name)." Look directly at your pupils; repeat this with all power and authority. Now, you must be thinking *she has lost it, having me stare in some mirror talking to myself, out loud.* Well, as a matter of fact **I have lost *it*.** I need you to lose *it too*…the, *it* of self-doubt and I can't do *it*. Please lose *it* so we can find and nurture the good stuff.

As business organizations, we must enhance and/or solidify our packages and responses. The package represents how we promote our business image, which is what we want our potential buyer to see. In short, how we are putting our stuff out there. Items that represent our package are the following: **resume, cover letter, thank you letters/notes, attire, mannerisms, grooming techniques and attitude**. I give packaging a 40% importance level for employability. Each of these items will be addressed as we move forward in our chapters.

The second and perhaps most important aspect of our business in terms of "salesmanship" is our response. Response is the *how* of how we sell ourselves and how we respond to questions, scenarios (verbal and non-verbal) and the sale of our products. This is the bread and butter of employment. When we are in the hot seat (a.k.a., the interview) the buyer is analyzing our every move, gesture, eye contact and expressions. It is imperative that we know how to express ourselves…market our skills, knowledge, abilities, and positive non-verbal communication to get the buyer to accept our bid. Now that I have you in the business focus, let's move directly to our response concepts and begin with the power of interviewing.

The Interview
(The Sales Meeting)

Power Statement No. 18

When you know the answers, the tough questions are easy.

—Mr. Robinson, 1998

What are those magical answers that hypnotize the interviewer to allow him/her to finally realize you are the right person for this job? What is the secret you may ask to hit those hard to reach questions? Well here it is. Not only is it important to have an idea of the possible questions, which we will provide to you, but you must also be well versed in your knowledge of self in order to respond effectively. The short story: you must know who you are and what you bring. Earlier we talked about self-inventories and how important it is for you to take the time to get real and confess, learn, and discover your strengths and limitations. Consider this a purification project—a time to peel away all those masks and lies (yes I said it...lies) that keep you from realizing your true purpose. I am going to act as if you have begun your self-inventory with an understanding that you have at least faced your goods and not-so goods.

I know you are waiting for the goods, so here they come. I have listed for you several anticipated questions that I have gathered from human resources agencies, managers and in my own experience in recruitment. I don't have the corner market on interviewing questions, nor does any other author for that matter. So I highly recommend that you research other books and/or articles for additional questions to increase your knowledge base. Nevertheless, here are some generic problematic interview questions:

Problematic Interview Questions

1. Tell me something about yourself?

2. Why should I hire you?

3. What are your strengths, your weaknesses?

4. What are your salary expectations?

5. Why did you leave your previous employer?

6. What would your last employer say about you?

7. What are your future plans, short-term and long-term goals?

8. Why do you want to work here?

9. Can you explain why you have been out of work for so long?

10. What did you like least/best about your previous employer?

11. How does your previous experience relate to this job?

12. Convince me in 60 seconds or less that you are the right person for this job.

13. What questions do you have for me?

Now, the interview process is not going to stop there. We are finding that organizations are also using what is called behavioral interviewing to not only access key skills, but to see how you use logic and processing skills. I am finding that this method is used in addition to the above generic questions. As suggested by Managing People at Work, here are six categories and questions to assess the key skills that organizations are looking for.

1. Initiative and Follow-through

    a. Describe a project or challenge that you've faced and how you overcame it?

2. Flexibility

    a. Describe a major change in your professional life and how you responded to it?

    b. Which change did you not agree with, if so, why?

    c. Did you find it easy to be effective or was it a struggle?

3. Team work

    a. Describe your relationships (work related activities) with past or current co-workers.

4. Business Sense

    a. Describe how your past employers met their business objectives?

    b. Who were their customers?

    c. What market segment did they target?

    d. What were the important features of their products?

    e. How did their work affect the organization's results?

5. Creativity and Problem Solving

    a. A hypothetical situation: You have been given a project to complete in 60 days. At the 45-day mark, 2 key team members are not available due to injury. Define the problem and share how would you handle this situation.

6. Self-development

    a. Identify something that you have learned in the last week?

    b. How did you learn this thing?

    c. When was the last time you deliberately sought to learn something new?

    d. What was the subject and how did you do?

Now, please understand that these exact questions may not be asked, but rest assured the categories will be the focus. Let's look at them for a moment to find out what organizations are looking for.

Power Statement No. 19

Remember the five P's-poor planning prevents peak performance.

—Rev. Scott, Sermon, 1999

Initiative and Follow-through: Organizations want to know if you finish what you start. Are you a quitter (victim) or do you press on (victor). In order to answer this question, you have to know for yourself if you are a quitter or a finisher. Now if you are a quitter, you need to find the desire to *do something different*. Find a small project to work on, initiate a plan, keep it simple, and follow it through. Take small steps. Don't try to solve the Middle East peace process, but maybe something more personal like completing this book. The bottom line is, an organization is not going to risk the investment in you if they get a faint hint that you won't invest in them.

Power Statement No. 20

A tree that won't bend in the wind will break.

—Ms. Brown, 1998

Flexibility: I hear it all day long when I am interviewing. "I am very flexible." Organizations ask that same question in a narrative way. Though people claim to be flexible, all day long they see, hear and feel "Oh no, I am not doing that!" This is a skill that could make or break you in terms of a hiring decision. Technology has changed the workforce and flexibility is a key element. If you are a person who is very rigid and requires a lot of structure and daily regimen, you have two options. The first, find industries that meet your structure and rigid requirements and only pursue those organizations during your employment search.

The second, and least restrictive method, get over it! It is important to identify areas in your professional world that will have difficulty with change management. Examples of this could be childcare, eldercare or family issues that could affect work hours, travel requirements and the like. My opinion is outside of those, everything else can be positively negotiated for flexibility and a win-win solution.

Power Statement No. 21

Can't we all just get along?

—Rodney King, Los Angeles riots

Teamwork: What else can I say, the days of being the isolated worker in your own little space is over. Should we thank technology for that? Your ability to work well with staff and associates is critical. Organizations are looking for members who can cooperate, give positive feedback and get the job done. If you have these skills, great, they will get you far. If you are *working on it*, I will give you a push-up in the right direction. Teamwork doesn't mean a bunch of buddies sitting and discussing stuff. It means working together in a positive fashion to get the job done. If you can do that, say it in your interview.

Power Statement No. 22

Always remember this, rule No. (1), No Outcome, No Income.

—**Walter Overfield, 2000**

Business Sense: Oh yes, the almighty dollar. Let's not be dismayed, we live in a capitalist society, which is fueled by the *Benjamin's*. How well you can convey your sense of understanding *the bottom line* can be a crucial victory on your road to employment. Every position is essential in an organization in order to keep the products delivered, keep customers satisfied and returning for additional business services. Organizations need associates who understand, and act on, the nature of business. If your business savvy needs a little work: that's okay. Decide how you are going to improve your knowledge base. To have zero business knowledge is not an option. Keep it simple, think about your own life scenarios. Rule 1: no outcome, no income. Rule 2: expenses should be less than income. Rule 3: if there are any disputes, refer to Rule 1.

Power Statement No. 23

Hope for the best, plan for the worse.

—**John Suffern, 2001**

Creativity and Problem Solving: Organizations are more impressed with how you work through a challenge and not just the outcome. Don't misunderstand what's being said; a solved problem is a great thing. However, the skills you use to identify, obtain data, make an assessment, gather resources, implement a plan, and evaluate your plan are *worth more than rubies* in today's workforce. These steps are also known as the "Problem Solving Method" (Hepworth and Larsen, 445). Be prepared for scenario questions such as the one identified on the previous page. If you are an expert problem solver, and can cite several examples of how you did it, great. However, if problem solving is not one of your strong suits, take the plunge with any smaller situations you can find that is important to your lifestyle. Prior to your job search, use the problem solving method to conquer any of these potential barriers to employment: childcare resources, transportation options, having to be in (2) places at the same time. Work/life issues, if presented correctly, can not only showcase how you use your problem solving skills, but also reinforce how ready you are for the workforce.

Power Statement No. 24

You Are Your Most Important Resource.

—Tonnie G. Harrison, 1991

Self Development: Do you want me to keep it real? In my humble opinion, organizations are assessing how devoted and invested you are to your own professional development. In other words, are you expecting the employers to solely foot the bill? Additionally, they may be assessing your learning style to see if it is compatible with the organization's personality. You must be able to sell how much you have invested in your professional goals (i.e. education, training, seminars) to remain a vital force in your area of expertise. If you have, great...simply tell your tale of your annual conferences, monthly meetings, etc. If you are struggling in that area, push-up, get on track and start learning something new today. Go to your local library; a book is a good thing and newspapers are okay. Reduce your television intake because television keeps you in a reactionary versus participatory mode. We are fed information from television. We are not able to engage in the learning process, which is necessary to stimulate the critical thinking and learning environment. At least with books or other literature, we can read several opinions, make up our own minds and discuss those thoughts with others. Wait, I am not writing a book about Reading is Fundamental; however, start thinking like this: "What have I learned today?" If the answer is nothing, read a book.

Your Shield, Do You Have a Breast Plate?

Power Statement No. 25

If you can conceive it, you can achieve it.

—Ms. Buckley, my 4th grade teacher 197?

The next item that I will present before you is part of your armor of protection. Any good warrior needs a strong outer shell to protect his/her most vulnerable organs. In the case of the breastplate, it is used to protect that trunkal area which encompasses our heart. Paraphrasing of course, the Bible tells us to put on the whole armor of GOD prior to battle so that we may be properly equipped. As an employment-seeking soldier, are you protected from the slings and arrow that are waiting for you? Are you covered with an outer garment to protect those most sensitive areas? Have you done your push-ups to get those weakened areas into their functional best? If your answers are anything but a strong and purposeful "Yes" then let's go to work!

The shield exercise is an activity that I have used during employability seminars and it has a two-fold purpose. The first purpose is to have a dynamic way of responding to the most common first question in an interview: "Tell me something about yourself." Secondly, it is a tool used to foster creativity, identify strengths, recognize limitations, categorize work history/experiences, announce accomplishments and initiate a professional rapport. An added bonus is that you will feel awesome and really put your interviewer on notice that you are an able and ready candidate.

Making My Shield
(It's Art Time.)

Power Statement No. 26

Just Do it!

—Nike, date unknown

The shield's structure is very simple and requires you to step out of your box and use the artistic expression that personifies your spirit. Yes, I am tapping into your artistic developments and I require the following: paper, pencil, crayons or magic marker and your imagination. Whatever symbol you come up with is fine. I have seen shields in the form of animals, homes, flowers, the cross, etc. Use your imagination; think to yourself, if I could pick one symbol to represent me it would be

_____.

Once you have determined your shield representation, the next step is to divide it into 5 areas and label them counter-clockwise 1, 2, 3, 4, and 5. Each of those compartments will be used to identify/respond to an area of questioning during the interview/marketing phase of your employment search. Below is a list of fill in the blank questions that corresponds with your shield and introduces its core concepts.

1. I am originally from _____.

2. I consider myself to be _____.

3. My work experience consists of _____.

4. I enjoy _____.

5. I am really proud of the fact that _____.

Our next step is to fill in the missing areas for each of the five categories on the sections of our shield representations. I know you are saying, "there is not a lot of space in here to write all of my information." You are correct, we do not need a large amount of text; I want you to find symbols to help trigger your mind towards the response. I have included an example of my shield in the appendix for you to get an idea of what I am asking you to do. No, I have not lost my mind; if you complete this exercise using the symbols and artistry that I have asked, you will find that you can remember your shield quickly, accurate and that it will be packed with power.

Again, refer to my example as we discuss the elements of each category. In the first box, write text or use symbols to respond to where you are from. If where you are is home, then state that. If you have relocated here, write the number of years you have resided or a symbol for the area. For example, I would draw a red apple to represent New York or a peach for Atlanta.

Box 2: Give me three words that describe you and write them in the box. I have included a list of descriptive words in the appendix section if you desire to use them. Now, this is the time to get real and accept your description of yourself. Toot your own horn; it's okay to enjoy and to shout the positive qualities that you hold. I would even go a step further. Use the first three words that you come up with. Sometimes, when we think about things too long, we change them. I say go with your first instinct.

Box 3: Take a quick picture of your last ten years of knowledge, abilities and skill (k.s.a.). Classify your three areas of expertise in terms of all your work history. This will give you a broader picture of "What you can do versus where you have been." For example, let's say I have worked as a sales associate for three years, an entry-level office clerk for two years, a car salesperson for six months and home childcare worker for seven years. Now, let's concentrate on the industry versus job category for this particular example. I would place in box three the following: 3.5 years in sales (retail/automotive setting), two years in administrative services, and over seven years in child development. Remember the emphasis is industry versus job title.

Box 4: This will include a snapshot of your human qualities. If you have hobbies or interests that are *appropriate* for disclosure and can assist in your professional development then state them. My experience has been that it's a good thing to be human during the interview process. It helps us stand out from the robots and the other competition. Here is an example: reading, writing and leadership activities. My only caution here would be to refrain from sharing items regarding political, faith-based (unless you are interviewing in a faith-based organization) or other activities that may not be *appropriate* for the workplace. As the mature people say, when in doubt, do without.

Box 5: Now this is your goal-oriented section. Think of items that you have accomplished that have made you proud. This can be a personal achievement, professional reward or acknowledgment. We all have accomplished something; now is the time to start thinking about it. Now, I will forbid one response, your children. Most of the women that I have worked with in the past have always said, "I am proud of my children." Don't shoot me, I think that's great, but don't you think that's a given? Aren't most parents proud of their children anyway? I want you to find something that is just for you. If you won employee of the year or sales person of the quarter—great. However, some of you have completed an educational program, are happy with the person that you have become or are proud of the fact that you are interviewing with this company today. All of the above are known as accomplishments, and it's okay to say so.

Using My Shield.

Power Statement No. 27

Take a healthy risk.

—**Mr. Franklin, 1997**

Now that you have made your breastplate creation, a symbol of your spirit with its artistic delights, you are ready to take your armor into battle. I recommend that you take some time to study your shield, so the compartments can become *flesh to you*. Not only is it important that you are able to recite your shield at a moments notice, but that you must believe what you are saying. As I stated before, if you don't buy it, why should we? Believe in yourself, in fact in many cases this is the chief reason one is hired and why one is not.

Using my shield as a guide, located in the appendix, when that first question is asked ("Tell me something about yourself"), here is the way you should respond:

> I am originally from Connecticut, but have lived in Virginia Beach now for 10 years. I consider myself to be a results-oriented, solution focused and committed individual. My professional experience consists of three years in management, five years in workforce development services and two years in direct practice. My interests are reading, writing and leadership activities, and I am very proud of the fact that I have received several awards based on my work performance.

Wow, imagine the response you will get and how you will drive the interview process if you start off on this good foot. Whenever someone challenges you on your work history with questions such as:

- Why should I hire you?

- What do you bring to the table?

- Tell me your chief strength and why?

- What skills do you feel are important to be successful here?

When asked, you can simply refer back to blocks 2, 3 & 5. Now, is our shield perfect right now? Of course my answer is not quite. It's enough for this practice exercise (and initial interviews) but I recommend having at least 10 words to describe yourself, (that you can fluidly interchange), and examples of projects or generics duties associated in the categorized work industries. For example, in my "five years in workforce development" it included projects such as: job develop-ment, cold calling, marketing clients, developing employment partners, conduct-ing training workshops/seminars, etc. I am prepared to discuss those specifically if asked by the interviewers because I have practiced them and attached them to my shield. A wise person once said, "Success equals opportunity plus preparation." In fact, after writing that statement, do I really need to say another word?

Sales and Marketing, That's The Name of the Game.

Power Statement No. 28

Feel the fear and do it anyway.

—Ms. Jones, 1997

When we get right down to it, everything is retail. We purchase goods/services keeping our eye out for price, quality and customer service. Be not dismayed, employers are shopping for the same things. They are comparing prices, looking at the package, evaluating history, determining whether or not they can get a bang for their buck. Why not give it to them, the bang I mean. Here are a few tips. Do the following…now.

Blow your own horn!

Did you notice that I did not say it's okay to blow your horn? I said just simply blow it. In your private spot, I want you to start shouting in full voice those 10 positive words that you have found that describe your essence and embrace your spirit. Think on, and believe, all of the great works that have come from your hands. Look at yourself in the mirror and smile; isn't it great to know that you are all right. The way you feel now, your internal passion needs to come across full force in that interview chair. Sell that.

Closing the sale: "and the winner is…"

You've believed in yourself, used your shield, applied retail dynamics, shouted your horn, your package and response is *tight,* now you must close the deal. Yes, remember my previous phrase "everything is retail?" As sales professional, it's time to seal the deal. Here are my recommendations: allow no more than 48 hours to pass between your interview and a thank you letter or note to the person(s) who would be making the hiring decision. Of course, when the interview ended you asked for a business card of the person(s) who interviewed you so that you can have a record of the meeting and important contact numbers. I will leave the presentation of your thank you entirely up to you. You may professionally type a standard letter, personalized of course, or a hand written thank you on a professionally looking note card. That should suffice.

The important thing here is sending a thank you in some fashion. You may be saying, "Why would I thank someone for a job interview when they have not offered me a job yet?" Remember the statement *act as if;* during all of your employer contacts, you must act as though you have received your blessings. You will present yourself as though you are the ultimate candidate. You will act as though this is the perfect match and as if you already have the job.

The thank you letter serves several functions that are paramount in the work-place. It demonstrates your ability to plan and organize. The thank you letter also showcases your courtesy and professionalism. While your competition will say all those routine words during the interview phase, you will demonstrate your exceptional gifts and professionalism by sending a thank you letter or note.

Second, remember how you felt when you received a thank you from a friend or colleague in response to a personal gesture? How did you feel, when you read how your gift or contribution meant so much to someone? Well, employers are people too. Everyone likes to hear a thank you from time to time.

The Thank You (An Example of Class)

A format or suggestion for your letter follows, but I really want you to express your sincere gratitude for having the meeting. Don't fall into the production-oriented trap; make this letter count. You may cite a particular statement that really meant something to you in your letter or emphasize how impressed you were with the interview and overall environment of the organization. The key here is to keep it simple, effective and real. Remember, people can tell when you're pouring *it* on too thick. A suggestive format for this letter/note follows on the next page:

Thank You Letter Example

DATE

Mrs. Francina R. Harrison
456 Motivation Drive
Purpose, VA 33333

Mr. Ican Doit
PUSH-UP Inc.
123 My Dreams Avenue
Positive, VA 11111

Dear Mr. Doit:

I would like to take this opportunity to thank you, and the panel, for the opportunity to interview for the (**name of position**) with the (**organization**). As I stated in the interview, this is an exciting opportunity for (**name of industry**) professionals and I would like to be a member of such a forward thinking initiative. I do believe my knowledge, skills, and can do personality will be an asset to your team. Again, thank you for your time, and I hope to hear from you soon.

Sincerely,

Francina R. Harrison, MSW

As you can see, this thank you is short and sweet. Remember the point of this is to make a lasting impression, showcase your professionalism, and demonstrate your leadership/initiative abilities. Just adding this touch to your job search plan can work wonders.

Closing The Sale....

Now you have discovered that your salesmanship is ready to go a step further and you have revisited your confidence/competence levels. I suggest you call the employer after you have mailed the thank you letter. Now this is a very tactful area and the *art* of salesmanship should kick in. The goal is to be persistent, not pushy, assertive not aggressive. This can be gauged by assessing the feeling or rhythm of the organization...its culture and personality. If none of that works, and you would like to use this approach, simply ask the interviewer if you can contact him/her. That will work every time. My experiences with this technique occurs during the closing portions of the interview. I ask the question "When do you expect to make a decision?" "May I call you on **that date** to discuss the position further?" If you receive a flat out no, pull back, send your thank you and leave it alone. However, if contact is okay, send your thank you, wait one (1) day, then follow up with the closing call. It could go something like this:

> "Mr. Doit, this is Francina Harrison, just calling to make sure that you have received my thank you letter...great! Have you made your decision?"

If the response is yes, gracefully end the call and be patient. If the response is other than yes, gracefully use the next 20 seconds to deploy your mini-sell and eagerness to work there, etc. Remember the key here is the *art* of job search. Don't shoot yourself by being too eager; however, definitely display how you are the best.

Telephone Techniques
—(A personal relationship with the telephone.)

Power Statement No. 29

Are you shy, well...get over it...phase I.

—**F.R. Harrison, 1997**

Congratulations! You have just met your new best friend, the telephone. Focusing on your marketing aspects, it's important to develop and sharpen your telephone technique. This is a new approach, but for me it has been most successful. By simply using the telephone, you can increase your job search results by 30%. Why is this technique so effective? It will save time, save gas, build your confidence level; help you develop your network and networking skills. Most employers prefer not to advertise. They would rather use employee referrals and networking, prior to placing an expensive advertisement. Understanding that, using the telephone as your legwork, you can tap into those unadvertised jobs, meet managers and research your chosen field by simply letting your fingers do the walking. Let's get started.

Power Statement No. 30

If you do what you always did, you will get what you've always got!

—**Strive Video, 1998**

As stated above, it's time to let go of the old and take on the new. For many people, calling employers on the telephone may feel at best a little awkward. Here I am asking you to make cold calls to employers who have no idea that you exist and make your sales pitch. Sure, you could think of many excuses why you should not do this. Below is a list of the most famous excuses for not cold calling:

- What if they hang up on me?

- What if they are busy?

- I don't want to bother anyone.

- I don't want to do that.

If you are honest with yourself and really feel that this is something you adamantly don't want to try, please refer to the power statement above. We don't want the same results, we want to tap into our power and find that which is ours. Looking for that fit will require you to step out of your bubble, test faith, stop making excuses, and accept responsibility. Take a healthy risk. You can do this. Now is the time to try something different.

Power Statement No. 31

F.E.A.R = False Evidence Appearing Real.

—Dr. Benjamin K. Watts, Sermon, 1991

If you have gotten this far in this reading, I think you know my position on fear. Yes, this is new, yes it's scary...so what? Most new things are scary, until you do them the first time. It's okay to feel the fear; it's okay to start breathing heavier when a new opportunity comes to you. Its okay to sweat, cry even...just don't let those physiological outbursts keep you from forward movement. Cry before and after your *new thing* if it makes you feel better. What's the bottom line here? Don't let your self-imposed fear cripple your potential future. When you allow fear to order your steps, your directions, your future, you have failed at the very essence of life.

A small step is much better than no step. Find your power avenues to build you up. You need that in order to make it to the next step. I know this writing is about your career pursuits, but can you see how using these steps, facing your fears, and trying something new is effective in all of our life deployments? You have got to move to get somewhere. I challenge you to take and make the next move. I dare you to discover what you are made of.

Telemarketing for Your Corporation.

Power Statement No. 32

Are you shy, really...well get over it, phase II.

— **F.R. Harrison, 1998**

We are all aware of telemarketers and how persistent and determined they are to get their sales. Yes, they call at the most awkward times, and yes, they can get on your last nerve. Do you know that those persistent buggers are one of the most effective methods of generating sales revenue for many major corporations and organizations? It's also one of the most cost effective methods of sales in terms of the bottom line. As with everything else in life, let's eat the meat of the telemarketing world and let's leave the bones behind.

What makes them so effective? In my opinion here it is:

- They know who you are, where you live, and they have your correct number.

- Telemarketers know the products that you have purchased in the past.

- They have a prepared script that has been rehearsed and tweaked to perfection.

- They are prepared for all possible outcomes.

- They look at the word *no* as an opportunity and not the end.

- Telemarketers are willing to make the sale easy for you.

When you think about it, these are some pretty incredible skills to have. Now here is the question for you, "Are you ready to telemarket yourself to the employer?" Use the same preparation skills listed above to ensure a sale. We are going to incorporate the above traits into your custom job search. From this moment on in your job search, you are a telemarketer; let's make your telemarketing work.

Power Statement No. 33

To thine own self be true.

—**William Shakespeare**

First Question: Where Do I Want To Work?

The question you must ask yourself is "Where do I want to work?" We have to research and discover your market. Based on your job skills, transferable skills, volunteer experience, interests, attitudes, hobbies, preferred environments; you need to identify viable companies and/or organizations that meet your standards. What do I mean? Here is an example: Let's say that I have the following administrative skills: clerical, office environment and computer savvy. I prefer to work 2nd shift hours (not a morning person). My interests include coaching, outdoor fun, and children. My personality is outgoing, creative, having fun and working with groups more than individuals.

Now, the next task is finding what industries (not job titles) would best suit my personality, interests, job skills, and work/life balance. There are several sources that you can use to help identify employers/industries. Generic examples are often at your area libraries, school placement offices and state employment offices. Since I love research, my first choice is always the library. Everything you need is right there and it's free.

Library sources I would search would be the following: chamber of commerce members (get an idea of what is available in the area), economic development commission (labor market info) and my favorite source, the local yellow pages. Yes, you read that right, the yellow pages. Simply put, the yellow pages are a list of every bona fide business and non-profit organization in the local area, a.k.a. potential employers. Keeping in mind the above example, I would use the yellow pages index (often in the rear of the book) to identify the above areas that interest me: (child, youth recreation/health care centers, clubs, recreation centers, sports.) For example, you will notice that when you search *child* you should find an infinite list of areas. You will then start the perusal process to see what interests you. This is an excellent activity for your journal.

They Know Who You are, Where You Live, and They Have Your Correct Number (Develop Your Market)

Next step, when you turn to those pages that interest you, make a photocopy of the entire page for each area of interest. This will provide for you the address, telephone number, copy of advertisement, and all contact information for future reference. In short, if you have five areas of interest and each page would have a list of 20 businesses, in this one step you could have over 100 potential *job leads* from this one technique. Perform this for all your interests whether they are job related or not. Find what interests you.

Telemarketers Know the Products That You Have Purchased in the Past

Yes, we are still in the research phase, but trust me if you do more quality focused work on the front end, it will save you the stress, which results from the *quick, fast and in a hurry* syndrome. Once we have identified at a minimum those 100 potential employers, let's use our thinking caps on the business expectations that they may need. Now if I found a summer camp listed, the likelihood that they would have year round work may be null. So again this is where the art of job hunting comes in. However, you know me, a phone call may still be necessary. It will let you know the actual versus the imagined.

In general, larger businesses have a need for the administrative, financial, customer services, direct services, sales, and operations staff. If you have identified what I call the Mom and Pop outfits, one person may perform several of the above roles or it may be family operated. That's okay, again this is the genesis of market research: to simply see what's out there and what the employers may need.

Power Statement No. 34

You must believe!

—*Houdini,* The movie

They Have a Prepared Script That Has Been Rehearsed and Tweaked to Perfection

Next step...time to make contact. We have identified organizations, brainstormed the business expectations, and are ready to perform our market research a.k.a. cold calling.

You must have a telephone script that will begin with the following words: who, when, where, how, what, in order to obtain the most information. The purpose of the contact is to determine the following:

- Who is in charge of hiring?

- What positions are they currently recruiting for?

- What type of person are you looking for?

- What is the application process (dates, times, hours)?

- How can a meeting be arranged?

Think of the initial contact as a fact-finding mission about the company. You are trying to gather as much information as possible within a five-minute phone call. Remember, I am a front-end heavy person. We are performing a lot of work before we even know if they are hiring. Keep reading. Let's see if you can guess what I am up to. There is a method to this madness.

Power Statement No. 35

Act as if…

—Jackie, last name unknown, 1999

I am going to give you sentence structures, open ended statements, opportunities to ask questions, pause or make a statement. All of this won't mean a hill of beans if before you get on the telephone; you have defeated your spirit with putrid self-doubt and self-defeating behaviors. If your mental tape is playing a victim song, sit down right now. Don't waste anyone's time. You have got to act as if you are going to be successful, going to get this job, going to let the world know you exist and claim your right to prosperity. You must act as if you are the right person for this opportunity. You must act as if they are sitting there waiting for that telephone to ring and to only talk with you. The first call will be the most difficult. I have been there, I have done this…I know the fear and anxiety. There is nothing special about me, just my ability to see pass the clutter, the fear and to embrace the future. I believe that you can do this, find the power in your spirit and do this. Remember, act as if…

The Cold Calling Techniques.

Always:

- Be courteous and patient to everyone you talk with (especially the administrative staff).

- Speak clearly and concisely.

- Be positive: give yourself a push-up!

- Smile over the telephone.

- Be persistent, but not pushy.

- Say thank you.

Ordered Steps (persistent approach)

1. Say "Good morning/afternoon/evening."

2. State your full name.

3. "Who is in charge of hiring?" Ask for the name of that person.

4. Ask to speak to that person.

5. Introduce yourself again with the appropriate greeting.

6. "What positions are you currently hiring for?"

7. "That _____position sounds interesting, can you tell me what you're looking for in the candidate?"

8. Listen to the response, take notes and identify important traits.

9. If asked, provide a mini-sell of yourself (your filet mignon). Remember to mention items listed in your note taking—if you have those skills.

10. "What is the application process?"

11. "I have a resume, may I fax or email it to you now?"

12. Say, "I am excited about this opportunity, thank you so much and have a positive day."

Hopefully, this will give you a taste of what is necessary for cold calling. I want you to include your flare, style and attributes. The above is simply a template; you must make it uniquely you. That comes in your self-discovery...which should be blossoming right about now.

There is an additional step you can take with the cold calling template if you want to push just a little bit more. As you can tell, I push the envelope and strongly suggest you make the effort. However, if you feel that a few push-ups are in order before you take the next step, I will understand. The extremely persistent approach follows:

Extremely Persistent Approach

11. "I have a resume, may I fax or email it to you now?"

12. "Mr./Mrs. _____, yes this is Francina Harrison, I wanted to make sure that you have received my documents?" "Great."

13. Restate mini-sell: "As you can see Mr./Mrs./Ms._____, I have over __ years in _____, a stable work history and the computer skills you are looking for."

14. Ask to meet—"This is a really great opportunity, is there a time when I can come out, meet you and discuss this opportunity in person?" "What is convenient for you _____?"

15. Reconfirm meeting date.

16. "Thank you so much for your time and I will see you on _____."

Tell me, what have we done here? Here is my take on it. We have just stream-lined your hiring process. We have cut through the traditional approaches of driving around town, filling out mountains of applications, waiting for callbacks, becoming frustrated and feeling stressed. We have met with a hiring authority, obtained the name of the individual, and obtained current employment informa-tion. If persistent, we have submitted our documentation and arranged for an interview! All without leaving our homes.

Imagine using this approach for all of your identified employment leads that you have found in your sources. As I said earlier, I load it heavy on the front end, but look at the end results. Each time you use this method, you will increase your self-confidence, enhance your communication skills, become more comfortable with your voice and reduce interview anxiety. Additionally, we are standing out from the crowd and demonstrating our leadership, initiative, internal motivation and results-oriented personality. We have said a whole lot, without opening our front door.

I know your next question. "What if they are not hiring? What if the first response to our question is 'no?'" Remember the telemarketer. One of their char-acteristics is that they see the word *no* as an opportunity. So should you. Here's what I mean:

The "No" Script

1. Say "Good morning/afternoon/evening."

2. State your full name.

3. "Who is in charge of hiring?" Ask for the name of that person.

4. Ask to speak to that person.

5. Introduce yourself again with the appropriate greeting.

6. "What positions are you currently hiring for?"

7. "We are not hiring" or hiring for positions that don't meet my skill set.

8. "Mr./Mrs. ____when do you anticipate hiring?" If no, proceed.

9. "Mr./Mrs. _____ I have really heard some wonderful things about this company." May I contact you again in say __ months to see if you are hiring in my field?"

10. "Thank you and have a wonderful day."

As you can see, it's all about future forecasting. You are still developing your networking skills, developing a rapport with the hiring manager, and building your self-esteem. Of course as with the yes scenarios, I have a more persistent *no* approach.

The *No* Script (Pushing the Envelope)

1. What positions are you currently hiring for?

2. "We are not hiring" or hiring for positions that don't meet my skill sets.

3. "Mr./Mrs. _____when do you anticipate hiring?" If no, proceed.

4. "Mr./Mrs. _____ I have really heard some wonderful things about this company. May I contact you again in say __ months to see if you are hiring in my field?

5. "Listen, I have a resume, which showcases my _____skills, computer aptitude and stable work history. May I fax or email this to you for your records in case something should become available?"

6. "Thank you for your time and I will talk to you soon."

Remember, you are the CEO of Me Inc. You must be willing to put yourself out there. Think of yourself as a business, believe in your abilities, and discover your talents. You can do all of this; you just have to make that commitment to yourself to do it. There is no reason not to be successful—personally and professionally. Believe in yourself, act as if you can do it, encourage yourself on a daily basis and surround yourself with like-minded friends/family. It's all up to you. Remember victim or victor, you choose.

The Resume
(Is What You See, What You
Get?)

Power Statement No. 36

Check yourself before you wreck yourself.

—**Young man, at a 7/11 Store, 1984**

Let's move on. We have built you up, discussed avenues for you to unlock your power and potentials, looked the fear factors in their faces, and decided to design our lives with a victor mentality. As in the previous portions of this book, if you are not feeling the above, then you must go back and re-read the previous chapters. Your self-commitment may not be strong enough yet to move on. I recommend more push-ups to make you stronger. Those that are ready, let's get going.

The resume is the marketing tool for your business. It is the advertisement to potential buyers who are submitting, request for proposals or RFP's for services. In the business world, competition exists, quantity is necessary, and quality is invaluable. We must create an effective marketing strategy that gets you noticed, reflects your outcomes, denotes your effectiveness, and gets you a telephone call for a personal meeting.

Where Do You Want To Go, How Do You Plan To Get There?

In our job search section, we talked about tapping into the hidden job market, using your telemarketing techniques, networking, developing a marketing script, closing the sale, and techniques to reduce your competition. We have defined our path, stated our goals, and now are ready to put our product on paper in order to open the doors. Your resume is the *door opener,* which is like the icing on the cake in terms of the career and life purpose goals. That is what your resume should do for you. Open the door for you to sell your goods and services to a prospective employer. Remember, all the heavy foundation work has been laid; now you have to build on it.

Can you see how all of this is coming full circle? You must decide who you are, discover your personal gifts/talents, announce those gifts and talents, define venues where your gifts and talents can shine, research those venues, and find the names/contact points for those venues while marketing yourself within those venues by finally making contact. If you keep your goals and objectives all on the same page, for the same purpose, on one accord, then that is a purposed filled, passion driven search plan for your life's work. Remember what I have said from the beginning, this is deeper than a job and it will begin and end with you.

The Brochure of Your Cooperation.

Let's really keep this simple. When we are looking to make a purchase, we shop around until that special something catches our eye. Once the item has caught our attention, we will ignore its immediate surroundings, look at it again, and in most cases pick it up. Let's focus on the pick it up part. Once we pick it up, we will then investigate to discover color, size, material and, of course, the price. After all of that scrutiny, we have a couple of choices: we will buy the item or return it to its rack. However, the most important part is that the item got picked up!

Think of the resume process in the same way. There are lots of items out there for the hiring managers to view. The trick of it is to have your product stand out and at least be picked up and considered…so let's discuss ways of how to get picked up!

Which Style Is Right For You

Before discussing what style is right for you, let me state what a resume is not. First of all, a resume will not get you a job. Its sole purpose is to get you an interview. If you have sent your resume out there and the fish are biting (the fish that you want to bite) then your marketing tool is effective. Second, the resume is not a book summation of your life. It is a marketing tool that should give a snapshot of your knowledge, skills, and abilities, emphasizing your strengths and minimizing your limitations.

I don't believe in reinventing the wheel so I won't give you the standard *here is the resume you should choose* filibuster. I know from my own research that there are literally thousands of resume books and resources in the market that can give you chapter, verse and examples. In fact I have included some great text as references if you should choose to get into the research mode. I know you are thinking, "Well then why does she have a section on resumes in this book if she is not going to tell me exactly what to do?" Well, I am glad you asked that question. I will never tell you what to do, merely give you some focus, reasoning strategies, and vision strengthening techniques to catapult you where you want to go. You want the short story? Your resume needs to compliment your life work vision. The language, action statements, accomplishments and presentation must reflect who you are and where you want to go. Choose whatever style is pleasing to you in terms of visuals. My main concern is that you have *meat* and not *fluff* when you put your resume out there.

I have attached some examples of the three main resume formats that are widely used in today's current job market. Remember style varies; however the three (3) most popular formats are: chronological, functional and combination. Here is the abridged version of when, who, and what situations are best served for each format. The chronological is the best choice for the job seeker who has a strong work history, almost no gaps in employment, and has experience as his/her main showcase. This format will always say, this is where I have been and what I have done, for those particular organizations (i.e., the 20-year AT&T employee).

The functional resume is the best choice for the job seeker who wants to say, *here's what I can do for you* versus *this is where I have been*. This format is a good choice for the job seeker that is entering/re-entering the work force, changing occupations, gaps in employment, new graduates or for persons who want to highlight all their functions not, just the ones that have been paid for (i.e. volunteer services, personal experiences, hobbies etc). In today's ever changing work climate, this format has been more accepted due to the demanding expectations of employers who require persons to have a myriad of skills and the ability to become a knowledge worker. The limitations of this format are that some traditional settings such as public services, are "red flagged" when they see this format which does not denote work history. Many times, employers infer a less than stable work history and possible retention problems.

The combination resume satisfies both needs for the job seeker who wants to say, *here's what I can do for you* and *here is where I have done it*. This format is by far my first choice for all the above job seekers (if applicable) and can be very successful in the workforce of today. This format is effective at minimizing limitations, emphasizing strengths, showcasing work history and provides an effective snapshot of who you are and what you bring (i.e., military, civilian, college students, professionals, managerial, laypersons). Again, let me repeat, *your resume style is your personal preference.* You decide the artistic measure. Just make sure that your format fits your vision.

RESUME EXAMPLES

Chronological Example 1.1

JANE DOE   **555.555.1212 (W)**
123 Anywhere Street   **555-444.1212 (H)**
Purpose, VA 121212   address@goes.here

OBJECTIVE: Rehabilitation Counselor

CAREER SUMMARY:

Multi-disciplined professional with over five years of experience in client based services and facilitation of specialty groups. Designed and implemented adult programming towards transition issues, community re-entry and work force re-entry for disadvantaged populations. Experienced in organizational development, project management, quality assurance, customer service, product development, market research strategic planning and meeting outcomes. Possess a cornerstone of social work knowledge and strategies, which facilitate individual movement from entitlement to empowerment. Ability to manage the co-existence of human service delivery, commerce and effective business practices. Exceptional communicator with polished presentation skills who hold an MSW from College State University

PROFESSIONAL EXPERIENCE:

2000–Present   **Project Manager**, COMPANY, Inc., CITY, STATE

Manage all aspects of business development and operations for a local office of the nation's leading provider of health, human services and technology to state and local governments. Provide training and counseling services under a $400k per year performance-based contract with City Department. Promoted to Project Manager from direct service staff within two years.

1998–2000   **Employer Services Specialist**, COMPANY, Inc., CITY, STATE

Facilitated therapeutic groups to job seekers enrolled in the City Welfare Reform initiative. Led city project in all areas of job development, job placements, and retention. Developed and maintained over 70 percent of project business and community partnerships. Effectively applied extensive clinical skills and practical knowledge to provide the highest quality of direct therapeutic services to assist clients towards self-sufficiency. Well versed in using the Internet and Microsoft office products. Member of several professional associations committed to work-force development.

1997–1998   **Clinical Social Worker**, COMPANY, Inc., CITY, STATE, Oversaw the daily functioning of the therapeutic community through teaching, advising, monitoring, role modeling, supporting and facilitating appropriate pro-ductive attitudes and behavior for a housing unit of 90 inmates. Facilitated inmate education through didactic sessions for 90 attendees. Assisted in the for-mulating of a positive culture and community while teaching the benefits of a drug-free/crime-free lifestyle. Provided individual and group counseling. Over-saw the jobs and duties of the program structure boards. Provided all case man-agement duties for 45 inmates. Maintained progress notes, treatment plans, evaluations, discharge summaries and other institutional related data. Responsi-ble for the programming of the community re-entry and transitional phases of treatment.

1996–1997   **Occupational Specialist,** COMPANY, Inc., CITY, STATE

Conducted labor market surveys. Coordinated all potential job leads and current labor market with counselor and client, in relation to client's transferable skills, physical capabilities and compensation expectations. Provided one-on-one coun-seling to clients. Acquired employment opportunities for clients via cold calling to Tidewater area employers. Able to work autonomously and organized my case-load and fieldwork duties with supervisor staffing occurring just once per week.

1996–1997   **MSW Social Work Trainee,** COMPANY, Inc., CITY, STATE

Maintained a caseload, which included inpatient and outpatient clients. Provided long-term case management and monthly follow up to patients assigned to Com-munity Care programs. As part of a treatment team, conducted assessments, pro-vided supportive counseling, assisted with final plans and provided comfort care for families and patients assigned to hospice care. Co-facilitated an intensive pro-cess group and provided individual supportive service for the Recovery Program. Assisted LCSW with case management and ongoing assessment of client recov-ery. Assisted with discharge planning and community referral services for Med/ Surg ward.

EDUCATION:

1997   Master of Social Work, College State University, College, VA
1995   Bachelor of Social Work, College State University, College, VA

Functional Resume 1.2

NAME
ADDRESS
TELEPHONE NUMBER

OBJECTIVE   To obtain a career opportunity in the **healthcare industry**.

SUMMARY OF QUALIFICATIONS

Over 15 years of solid work history, which showcases my work ethic and personal fortitude. Eight years of experience in pathology/laboratory services. Seasoned in all aspects of tissue preparation, handling, and classifications. Familiar with medical terminology and has worked in a healthcare management call center. Self-starter who eagerly accepts new challenges and manifests high personal standards. Eligible and pursuing certification for histology from the American Society of Certification Pathology Board. Over five years of providing quality customer services, is computer literate and can operate effectively in a Windows environment.

AREAS OF EFFECTIVENESS

Medical Care Management Skills

- Entered medical authorizations and responded to inquires from medical providers.

- Assisted providers and billing agencies with authorization and inquires.

- Performed duties as a resource agent to members, providers and staff.

- Provided medical claims research, eligibility, SSI status, denials, and appeals.

- Registered requests for specialist consultations and therapeutic evaluations.

- Utilized CPT, ICD-9 and DRG coding systems.

- Utilized medical management specific computer applications and databases.

- Entered patient data into medical system for billing purposes.

Technician Skills (Phlebotomy/Histology/Pathology Technician)

- Identified, recorded tissue samples (cener) and assisted pathologist in dissection of surgical specimens.

- Prepared slides of tissue for microscope examination.

- Dehydrated, embedded, cut, stained, decalcified and used frozen cryostat methods.

- Routinely used electron microscopy and immuofuloersce.

- Maintained filing and slide storage systems for local researcher.

- Used universal precautions and safe disposal of contaminated medical waste.

- Performed venipuncture procedures on damaged veins in hospital setting.

- Performed all duties associated with phlebotomy.

Customer Services/Administrative Skills

- Reconciled, maintained office checking account and performed duties as cashier for a major retail outlet.

- Greeted customers in a professional manner in person and over the telephone.

- Handled irate customers with tact, diplomacy and identified problems and proposed solutions.

- Operated office machinery, answered telephones and maintained files.

- Performed customer relation duties in an auto insurance call center.

- Provided customer account updates, cancelled policies and solved problems.

EDUCATION AND TRAINING

(1996–2002 attended various professional development seminars specific to healthcare)
1980   Medical Administration—80 credits, City College, City, State
1975   Bachelors Degree—Fashion Design, City College, City, State
1974   Diploma—Medical Administrative Assistant, City College, City, State

Combination Resume 1.3

NAME
ADDRESS
TELEPHONE NUMBER

OBJECTIVE   To obtain a career opportunity in the **healthcare industry** where my technical, business and customer skills can be used to our mutual benefit.

SUMMARY OF QUALIFICATIONS

Over 15 years of solid work history which showcases my work ethic and personal fortitude. Eight years of experience in pathology/laboratory services. Seasoned in all aspects of tissue preparation, handling, and classifications. Familiar with medical terminology and has worked in a healthcare management call center. Self-starter who eagerly accepts new challenges and manifests high personal standards. Detail oriented individual who exceeds expectations while delivering quality services. Eligible and pursuing certification for histology from the American Society of Certification Pathology Board. Over five years of providing quality customer services. Computer literate and can operate effectively in a Windows environment.

AREAS OF EFFECTIVENESS

Medical Care Management Skills

- Entered medical authorizations and responded to inquires from medical providers.

- Assisted providers and billing agencies with authorization and inquires.

- Performed duties as a resource agent to members, providers and staff.

- Provided medical claims research, eligibility, SSI status, denials, and appeals.

- Registered requests for specialist consultations and therapeutic evaluations.

- Utilized CPT, ICD-9 and DRG coding systems.

- Utilized medical management specific computer applications and databases.

- Entered patient data into medical system for billing purposes.

- Requisition supplies and maintained inventory for histology laboratory.

Technician Skills (Phlebotomy/Histology/Pathology Technician)

- Identified, recorded tissue samples (cener) and assisted pathologist in dissection of surgical specimens.

- Prepared slides of tissue for microscope examination.

- Dehydrated, embedded, cut, stained, decalcified and used frozen cryostat methods.

- Routinely used electron microscopy and immuofuloersce.

- Maintained filing and slide storage systems for local researcher.

- Used universal precautions and safe disposal of contaminated medical waste.

- Performed venipuncture procedures on damaged veins in hospital setting.

- Performed all duties associated with phlebotomy.

Customer Services/Administrative Skills

- Reconciled and maintained office checking account.

- Performed duties as cashier for a major retail outlet.

- Greeted customers in a professional manner in person and over the telephone.

- Handled irate customers with tact and diplomacy.

- Identified problems and proposed solutions.

- Operated office machinery, answered telephones and maintained files.

- Performed customer relation duties in an auto insurance call center.

- Provided customer account updates, cancelled policies and solved problems.

EDUCATION AND TRAINING

(1996–2002)	Attended various professional development seminars specific to healthcare)
1980	Medical Administration—80 credits, City College, City, State
1975	Bachelors Degree—Fashion Design, City College, City, State
1974	Diploma—Medical Administrative Assistant, City College, City, State

PROFESSIONAL EXPERIENCE

2002–2002	**Preauthorization Assistant**	Company, City, State
2002–2002	**Sales Assistant**	Company, City, State
2001–2002	**Histology Technician**	Company, City, State
1992–2001	**Histology Technician**	Company, City, State
1990–1992	**Phlebotomist**	Company, City, State
1986–1990	**Customer Service Assoc**.	Company, City, State

Resume Check Off/Review

Let's review a moment regarding the importance of your resume. In all actuality, the resume is your first work sample for an employer. This will be the first product you *put out there* and as I said before, this brochure is representing you. You must make sure that you have initiated the proper use of the English language, grammar, punctuation and spelling. I recommend that you have your resume reviewed no less than three times. I prefer to review it first, and then allow a friend or family member give me an objective opinion. This will ensure that your brochure is communicating the items that you want. If you are the only one available then try the following: First draft, wait one hour. Second review, wait one hour. Finally, review a third time. Once you have done those two suggestions, I have included a check off list that will give you a tangible tool to make sure you have dotted the *I's* and crossed the *T's*.

Is It Flesh To You?

Are you thinking that I have lost it at this point? That I am really taking this job thing just a little too deep and now I have suggested, that you eat your resume. Something that becomes flesh to you is a part of you. It's digested in your system; you have consumed it with a hunger and passion for survival. You know the raw meat stuff. So, yes I am suggesting that you eat your resume. In fact, you should have every word of your resume tattooed on both halves of your brain so that your can sleep it, dream it and quote it on point. You must be able to interpret, explain, elaborate, react and sell your marketing tool without hesitation. The words or grunt "uh..." is no longer acceptable or allowed. If you don't know your product inside and out, how can you expect that someone else will? You must be ready for any questions that may come up. No excuses, no denial, no drama. This is all on your shoulders.

Power Statement No. 37

Victor or victim, you choose.

—1995

In The End, It's All About You!

Have I scared you a little? Made you a bit uneasy, destroyed that comfort zone or your victim stance? Good, well here is some more kicking. Here is the question, "How am I going to learn all this stuff?" Here's my answer: study. Yes, your school is in session, and your life's work is on the line. What better subject to study than you? Just like in school, when a new subject matter was taught, we read out loud, took notes, memorized key points, listened actively and used repetition. Gather your like-minded friends and associates together to quiz you on your resume, interviewing skills, and possible questions. No friends? Fall in love with your mirror image and start talking to yourself. Look at how you respond when you read your resume. Observe your body language, your eye contact, and your smile. Remember, no victims here, stop blaming others for what you don't know. Those days are now over; your renewed focus is on you.

At this point, it's time for you to get in touch and process all the information I have shared with you. Prior to the reading of this book you may have been unaware of your behaviors, negative self-talk and defeating attitudes. What I have shared with you is not new; you have heard this before but just didn't listen. Now, there is no excuse for you not to meet your goals and you are aware of the expectations. In any case, now that you are aware that this is *deeper* than a job and it's all about you; you are now accountable for this new knowledge. It's time for your application stage where you get busy with your lifework and self-discovery. I am excited for you and expect great accomplishments in both your career and personal lives. It is finished; the torch of employability *knowledge* and *know-how* has been passed from me to you. This is your opportunity to make your life work. Give your self a push-up and a round of applause! Congratulations! You now have the spirit and *a mind to work*.

APPENDIX

Daily Power Statements for Living

Last but not least, I want to thank all of the people who have touched my life with verbal Power Statements listed throughout this book. Thank you for your wisdom.

1. If it's in the root, it's going to show up in the fruit.
    —William .D. Scott—Pastor Pleasant Grove Baptist Church, Sermon, Virginia 1998

2. Your attitude determines your altitude.
    —W.D. Scott, his words, 1995

3. A leader without followers is nothing more than a man taking a walk by himself.
    —Dr. W.D. Scott, his words, 1999

4. Making a living is not the same as making a life.
    —Rev. Moore, 1999

5. Knowledge is what you teach yourself, wisdom is what you learn from others.
    —Ettishia Goode, Retired Worker, Chesapeake Virginia, her words, 1999

6. When there is no wind, row.
    —Arthur unknown, 1999

7. Define yourself or be defined.
    —Diane Williams, occupation unknown, Chesapeake, VA, 1997

8. As a man thinks, so he is.
    —King James Version, *Bible-Proverbs*, 23:7

9. Get on top of your struggle.
    —Renee, coworker, Chesapeake, VA, her words, 1997

10. Handle your business.
    —Renee, her words, 1997

11. You have two guarantees in this world, one is life the other is death, what you do in between is totally up to you.
—Arthur unknown, 1992

12. I'm tired of surviving; I want to live.
—Donna, her words, 1997

13. Feel the fear and do it anyway.
—T. Jones, co-worker, Chesapeake, VA, her words, 1997

14. Walk like you have a purpose.
—K. Brown, coworker, Virginia Beach, VA, her words, 1998

15. The program works when you live it.
—Jackie, (name withheld), Virginia Beach, her words, 1998

16. Fake it to you make it.
—T. Jones, her words, 1997

17. How you react to a situation says more about you than the situation.
—Dr. Benjamin. K. Watts, Shiloh Baptist Church, New London, CT, Sermon, 1987

18. You are a reflection of your community.
—**Louis**, Virginia Beach, VA, 1997

19. Trust the process.
—Louis Smith, coworker, Chesapeake, VA, 1997

20. Take a healthy risk.
—Julius Franklin, previous supervisor, Chesapeake, VA, his words, 1997

21. The truth will set you free.
—Sanford and Son television series, date unknown

22. Can't keep it unless you give it away.
—T. Jones, her words, 1997

23. Comply then complain.
—Franklin, his words, 1997

24. If it don't apply, let it fly.
    —Joyce, her words, 1995

25. If you never ask the question, the answer will always be "no."
    —Robert, his words, 1998

26. Think before you act or react.
    —Sam, last name unknown, 1996

27. If nothing changes, nothing changes.
    —At the bus stop, 1996

28. There is no such thing as a free lunch.
    —Ms. Buckley, Winthrop Elementary School, New London, CT, 4th Grade, Her words, 197?

29. It takes more energy to keep quiet than to speak your mind.
    —Moore, his words, 1997

30. None are more hopelessly enslaved than those who falsely believe they are free.
    —Goethe, 1832

31. People will give you what you believe.
    —Moore, his words, date unknown

32. Decide who you are before deciding what you'll do.
    —Moore, his words, unknown

33. I am the CEO of Me Inc.
    —Byron Williams, Businessman, Virginia Beach, VA, his words, 1998

34. Reality is the best fantasy there is.
    —**Ms.** Burns, her words, 1999

35. The mind is its own place, and in itself, can make a heaven of hell or a hell of heaven.
    —Milton, 1608–1674

36. Will Power—if you don't have the will, you won't have the power.
    —Thelma (name withheld), her words, 1999

37. Know who you are and what you bring.
    —Dr. Joseph Dancy Jr., Classroom Lecture, Professor Norfolk State University, School of Social Work, Norfolk, VA 1995

Additional Resources for further Reading

Falcone, Paul. *96 Great Interview Questions to Ask before You Hire.* AMACOM Publishers, January 1997

Mahan, Brian J. *Forgetting Ourselves on Purpose: Vocation and the Ethics of Ambition,* Fairfax, VA: Jossey—Bass Publishers.

Pinkley, Robin L., and Northcraft, Gregory B. *Get Paid What you're Worth.* Griffin Trade Publishers. March 2003

Ryan, Robin *Winning Cover Letters,* John Wiley & Sons, October 2002

Whitecomb, Susan B. *Resume Magic: Trade Secrets of a Professional Resume Writer,* Jist Works Publishers. January 1999

References

Covey, Stephen R. *The 7 Habits of Highly Effective People.* New York, NY. 1989. Simon & Schuster.

Hepworth, Dean and Larsen, JoAnn. *Direct Social Work* Practice. Pacific Grove, CA. 1993 Brooks/Cole Publishing Company.

Managing People at Work. Round Rock, TX. October 1999. Professional Training Associates.

The Holy Bible, Revised Standard Version: New York. 1962. New American library.

Vanzant, Iyanla. *Acts of Faith: Daily Meditations for People of Color.* New York, NY. 1996 Simon & Schuster.

Webster Dictionary Online. www.webster.com 2003

Descriptive Words (just a start)

able	accurate	active	adaptable
adept	administrative	advantageous	aggressive
alert	ambitious	articulate	assertive
attentive	bilingual	broad minded	calm
candid	capable	diplomatic	disciplined
discreet	diversified	eager	easily
easygoing	effective	effortlessly	empathetic
experienced	loyal	meaningful	methodical
meticulous	motivated	open-minded	objective
orderly	patient	perceptive	persistent
persuasive	practical	risk-take	scope
self-confident	self-controlled	self-reliant	sharp
sincere	skilled	solid	specialized
stable	strong	substantial	successful

10 Point Resume Review/Checklist

- Run a spell check.

- Have at least (3) people review/proofread your resume.

- Use 8 ½ x 11 white or off-white professional stock paper.

- Use a font sizes between 10–14 point.

- Use one typeface and stick to it.

- Avoid italics, script and underlined words—difficult for scanners.

- Do not include information regarding age, religion or politics.

- Avoid using nicknames and non-professional email addresses.

- Use a workable telephone number with a professional message.

- Do not fold or staple resume—if mailed, use a large envelope.

My Shield Example

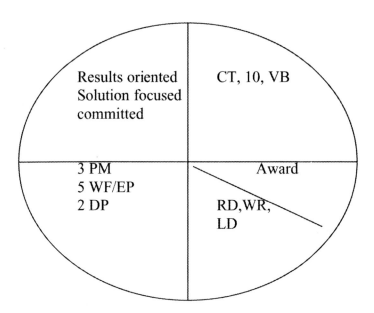

About the Author

Born in Kinston, NC, and raised in New London, CT, Francina R. Harrison's experience in occupational social work and life/career coaching has spanned more than 10 years. Her work has been instrumental in designing programs that help job seekers enter and remain in the workforce. Her program contributions have been successful in the following areas: welfare reform, correctional treatment, private vocational rehabilitation, and faith-based groups. Francina is the co-owner of a consulting business, Harrison & Associates, a freelance writer and conducts several workforce preparation seminars with her specialty being the transitional worker. The author is the mother of two children; a proud Navy Wife…married to a 20-year active-duty Navy service member and resides in Virginia Beach, VA. She holds a MSW (Master's Degree in Social Work) from Norfolk State University, Norfolk, VA. To contact the author directly or for further information on Harrison & Associates, please view the website www.thecareerengineers.com or send your emails to francinaharrison@thecareerengineers.com

0-595-30390-0